KT-425-357

WITHDRAWN
RESOURCE
SERVICE

2100025288

E.L.R.S.

Everyday Maths

Fun with food

Annie Owen

WAYLAND

S 355249

Everyday Maths

At Home
Fun with Food
Ourselves
Out and About

First published in 1995 by Wayland (Publishers) Ltd,
61 Western Avenue, Hove, East Sussex BN3 1JD

© Copyright 1995 Wayland (Publishers) Ltd

British Library Cataloguing in Publication Data

Owen, Annie
Fun with Food. – (Everyday Maths)
I. Title II. Series
510

ISBN 0-7502-1394-9

Printed and bound in Italy by Rotolito Lombarda, S.p.A., Milan
Design and typesetting by Can Do Design, Buckingham
Illustrations by Clare Mattey

Picture acknowledgements
Brian Armson 1, 5, 8 (all), 13, 14, 18, 20 (top); Karin Craddock
Cover, 6, 7, 10, 15 (all), 20 (bottom), 21, 23, 26; Greg Evans
International 22, 27; Sally and Richard Greenhill 12 (both), 24;
Christina Newman 9; Tony Stone Images 25.

Contents

Words in **bold** in the text are explained in the Glossary on page 28.

 This symbol shows there is an activity to be completed.

Our favourite foods

What is your
favourite food?
Why do you like it?
Do you know
someone with the
same favourite food
as you?

Ask your family and
friends about their favourite
foods. Make a **tally chart** like
this to record the answers.

Which food is the most
popular? How many people
chose it?

Food	Number who chose it
Pizza	////
Chips	//// /
Beans	///
Fish	/

Some foods are full of things that make us strong and healthy. Other foods have too much sugar, salt or fat in them. They are not good for us.

Talk about the good foods you eat with your family and friends. Ask each person to choose one good food.

Make a new tally chart to record the answers. Now make a **bar chart** like this:

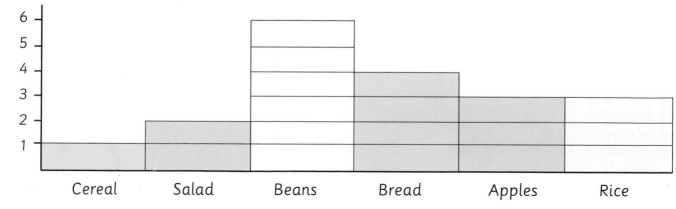

Delicious drinks

Look at these different bottles. Which one do you think holds the most water? What would you use to measure the water in each bottle? Why?

Find three different shaped bottles. Guess which one will hold the most water. Label it '1'. Guess which bottle will hold the least water. Label it '3'. Label the other bottle '2'.

Now measure the water each bottle holds. Put the bottles in order and write down their numbers. Were your guesses correct?

Make three drinks with fruit squash and water. Make one drink with 1 tablespoon of squash, one drink with 2 tablespoons of squash and one drink with 3 tablespoons of squash. Ask your friends which drink tastes the best. Write down the answers.

Measure how many tablespoons of squash are in a whole bottle of squash. Work out how many drinks you can make using 2 tablespoons of squash each time.

What time of day?

Some people eat their meals at different times of day. Marco eats his breakfast at eight o'clock in the morning. Some people eat breakfast earlier than this. Some people eat later than this. When do you eat breakfast?

When does Marco eat his lunch? When does he eat his dinner? How long is it between his lunch and his breakfast? How long must he wait between lunch and dinner?

Mr Jones is a postman. He has to go to work very early to deliver our letters and parcels. He gets up at half past five in the morning.

What time do you think Mr Jones has breakfast? Write down the times when you think he eats his meals. Draw a clock to show each meal time.

Draw clocks to show the times when you ate your meals yesterday. Can you write these times in numbers only?

Choose a pizza

Many people like to eat pizzas. Most
pizzas have more than one topping.
Look at these three pizzas. How many
toppings are there on each pizza?

 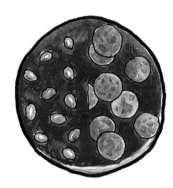 

A pizza base is a circle. Draw a
circle on some paper. Use a plate or
any round plastic shape to help you
do this. Cut out your circle.

Fold your circle in **half**. Open it
out and draw a line to mark the two
halves of your circle. It could be a
two-topping pizza with a different
topping on each half. How could
you make a four-topping pizza?

Use two circle shapes to make one two-topping pizza and one four-topping pizza. Draw the toppings on your pizza shapes. Write a list of your toppings like this:

> **Two-topping**
>
> ½ cheese
>
> ½ tomato

> **Four-topping**
>
> ¼ cheese
>
> ¼ tomato
>
> ¼ prawn
>
> ¼ onion

Look at the list of pizza toppings and the prices. Choose two toppings for a pizza that you would like to eat. Write down their names and the prices. How much would the toppings cost for your pizza?

La Pizzeria

Toppings:

onion	20p
cheese	25p
mushroom	50p
olives	40p
tomato	25p
prawns	50p

Ice-cream

Everybody loves ice-cream! You can have an ice-cream in a cone or in a tub. The biggest dishes of ice-cream are called sundaes.

Scoop ice-cream	50p
Wafer	20p
Whipped cream	30p
Nuts	20p
Chocolate flake	40p
Chocolate sauce	20p
Raspberry sauce	20p

You have £1 to spend on a sundae. What would you have in your sundae? If you had £1.50 what would you choose? Make a list with the prices. Use a calculator to help you check the cost of your sundae.

Jim sells ice-cream. He makes double cones which have two different flavours.

On Monday, he has strawberry, chocolate and vanilla ice-cream. He can sell three kinds of double cones.

On Tuesday, Jim has banana ice-cream as well. So he has four different flavours of ice-cream. How many kinds of double cones can he make now? Draw all the cones and label or colour them like these:

Sandwiches

Bread can be made in loaves of many different shapes and sizes. A sandwich loaf has square slices of bread.

We can cut the slices into halves or **quarters**. Here is one way to cut a square slice of bread into halves and one way to cut the slice into quarters.

Find some other ways to cut a square slice of bread into halves or quarters. Use some square pieces of paper to help you. Draw lines on each square to show how you would cut it up.

Sanjay is good at making sandwiches.
He has left instructions for his sister.
Sanjay has written one instruction on
each piece of paper. Miah has mixed
them up.

Look at the pictures and write down the
instructions in the right order. Is there more than
one way to do this?

Eat the sandwich

Cut in ½

Spread jam

Cut a ¼

Spread margarine

Put together

Eat a ¼

The picnic game

You will need:

2 dice with special labels (see p.30)

1 counter for each player

How to play:

1. Place all the counters on the picnic table.

2. Take turns to throw the dice.

3. Move your counter the number of squares shown on one die, in the direction shown on the other die.

4. If your throw would take you off the board, have another throw.

5. If you land on a square with food in it, write down the name of the food.

6. The first person to have the names of four different foods is the winner.

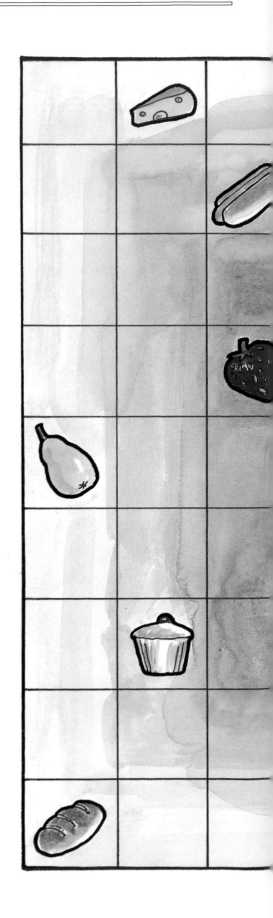

Making biscuits

When we make biscuits, we can use cutters to make them into different shapes. Do you know the names of these shapes?

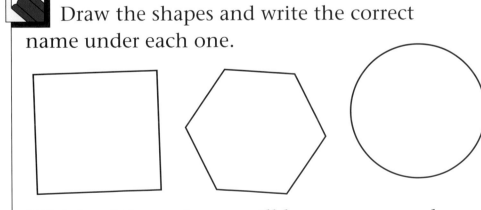 Draw the shapes and write the correct name under each one.

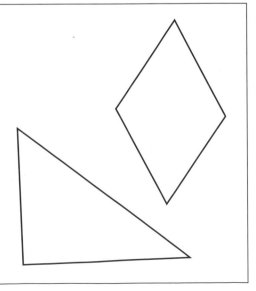

Which of these shapes will leave no gaps when the biscuits are cut out?

Look at the page from the cookery book. The recipe is for 15 biscuits. Write down the amount of each ingredient you will need to make 30 biscuits. You can use a calculator to help you.

Shortbread Biscuits

Makes 15

Ingredients:

100g butter

50g caster sugar

175g plain flour

Extra sugar for dusting

Cook at 150°

Cook in the oven for 30 minutes.

If the biscuits went in the oven at 4 o'clock, when would they be cooked? If you wanted the biscuits to be cooked by 3 o'clock when would they be put in the oven?

You will find the full recipe for the biscuits on page 31.

Food cartons

Many different kinds
of foods are put in
cartons.
Some cartons are small
and some are large.
They can be many
different shapes.

Collect five cartons. How many sides does each one have? What shapes are the sides? Choose one empty carton and open it out. Cut off the tabs. Put the carton on a piece of paper and draw round the edge. This is called the **perimeter**.

Choose two more cartons. Guess which one has the longest perimeter. Use string to check if your guess is correct.

Find three empty cartons. Hide different weights inside them. Put a letter on each carton. Ask a friend to guess which carton is the heaviest and which is the lightest by holding them. Check with a weighing scale. Did your friend get the cartons in the right order?

Fruit is fantastic

Fruits come in different shapes, sizes and colours. Some are soft and others are hard. Some have seeds inside them and others do not. Can you think of some other differences?

Draw a picture like this one with two labels – 'red' and 'soft'. Write the names of red fruits in the 'red' circle. Write the names of soft fruits in the 'soft' circle. Think of some fruits which are red and soft. Put their names in the middle.

Many fruits are **symmetrical**. This means that one side is the mirror image of the other.

Cut some fruits in half. Look at one half. Is it symmetrical? Draw the halves. Now draw the mirror line on each half.

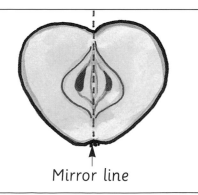

Mirror line

Growing food

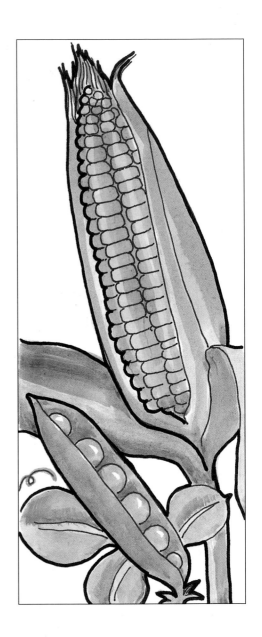

Michael lives in a small village. The
farmers near his village grow
sweetcorn and peas. These plants
grow from seeds. When we cook
sweetcorn and peas we are using the
new seeds or kernels. How many peas
are in this pea pod? Guess how many
kernels are on this corn cob.

Sweetcorn and peas both take about four months to grow. If we plant the pea seeds in March when will the new peas be ready to eat? If we want new sweetcorn in September, when should we plant the sweetcorn seeds?

Calendar

JAN	FEB	MAR
APRIL	MAY	JUNE
JULY	AUG	SEPT
OCT	NOV	DEC

Chen lives in a town. Her mother has a small garden. Chen grows flowers and herbs in her part of the garden.

Chen is going to plant some parsley seeds. The packet says 'Plant 20 cm apart' so Chen can grow 5 plants in one **metre** of ground. If she had 2 metres of ground how many parsley plants could she grow?

scale: 15cm = 1m

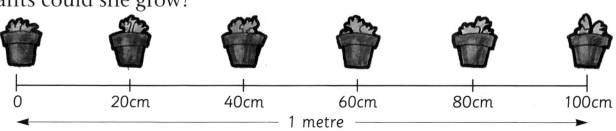

0   20cm   40cm   60cm   80cm   100cm

← 1 metre →

Keeping food cold

Some foods go
bad unless they
are kept cold.
A refrigerator is a
good cold place
to keep these
foods.

Talk to your friends and some adults
about where they keep different foods.
Draw your own food table like this:

Keep food cold in fridge	No need to put in fridge

Meat needs to be kept cold. The best **temperature** for keeping meat is between 0°C and 5°C.

We can keep foods in the freezer for a long time. The table below shows how long each food can be kept in the freezer.

Make a list to show the last month you could eat each food, if you put them all in the freezer today. Use a calendar to help you.

3 months

6 months

4 months

12 months

Glossary

Bar chart

A bar chart is a picture which records information. Each bar on the chart gives you two pieces of information. This bar chart shows you how many carrots each hamster has eaten.

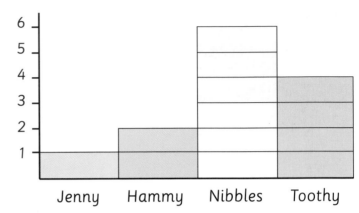

Calendar

A calendar shows how the days are arranged in each month of the year. Each year has a different arrangement.

Half

A half is written like this: ½. It tells you the object or number has been divided into two equal parts.

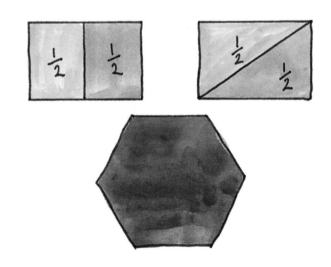

Hexagon

A flat shape with 6 sides.

Metre

A metre is a length we use for measuring large things. It is made of 100 centimetres.

Perimeter

The length around the edge of a shape.

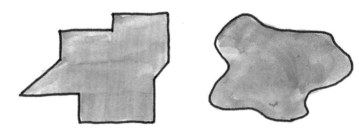

Quarter

A quarter is written like this: ¼. It tells you the object or number has been divided into 4 equal parts.

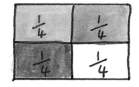
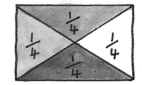

Symmetrical

A shape is symmetrical if it can be folded into halves and the two halves make a mirror picture of each other.

Tally chart

A way of recording the amounts which are being counted in groups of five. One line or mark is made for each item. The first four items are marked with straight lines. The fifth item is marked with a line that goes across the four straight lines.

Temperature

A measure of heat or cold. We use units called degrees Celsius. Water turns to ice at 0°C. When the temperature is colder than 0°C the degree has a 'minus' sign in front of it. -1°C is one degree colder than 0°C.

Notes for parents and teachers

Page 4/5

It would be helpful for children to discuss the questions they may ask in order to collect the information they need. Younger children who are just beginning to use tally charts can make straight marks in a line. However it is important to introduce the 'five-barred gate' method, as this will enable them to count their items more quickly.

Page 6/7

Young children often make assumptions about capacity of a container based on its height alone or its width alone. These activities enable them to realise that the situation is more complicated. Initially they should use non-standard measures such as egg cups, tablespoons etc. Then after a lot of practice, they could begin to use standard measures. Containers which hold ¼ and ½ litres are preferable as our units of capacity are difficult for children to understand and use.

Page 8/9

Wherever possible, situations such as writing daily diaries, reading stories at bedtime etc., should be used to introduce the concepts of time and the passage of time. It is important to talk about the difference which occupations can make to time – particularly if children have contact with shift workers and others in this position. The game 'What's the time Mr Wolf?' can be played with the 'wolf' holding up a toy clock face or a digital display, each time the question is asked.

Page 10/11

Folding can be done with any symmetrical shape e.g. a table napkin, or pieces of paper. String can also be folded to make fractions of length -– although only halves or quarters are recommended at this stage. Some children can extend the activity to thirds and later sixths. The pizza activities can be extended by altering the number of parameters. For example you could ask children how many pizzas they can make with 3, 4 and maybe 5 toppings.

Page 12/13

It is important to give children frequent opportunities to use and talk about money. The prices here have been chosen for ease of calculation. If the numbers are too large for a particular child to handle, model the prices with real or toy money. The double-cone puzzle produces the following results if two different flavours are always used: 2 flavours – 1 combination; 3 flavours – 3 combinations (shown); 4 flavours – 6 combinations.

Page 14/15

The simple ways of dividing a square into halves are:

The simple ways of dividing a square into quarters are:

The sequencing activity of making sandwiches will improve children's logical thought processes and concept of time. There may be more than one possible correct answer.

Page 16/17

This game will improve children's use of spatial directions, and reinforce their understanding of left and right. The 2 dice will need to be marked. One die should be labelled L, L, R, R, U, D. Make sure the children understand that these stand for Left, Right, Up and Down. The other die should be labelled 1, 2, 3, 1, 2, 3. The children throw both dice and move the number of squares thrown in the direction thrown. For example, U3 means move three squares up. They may need help the first time they play the game.

Page 18/19

Looking at shapes and patterns in school and at home and asking children to describe what they see happening is a useful introduction to tessellating shapes. If a pattern is made using only one shape, and if there are no gaps, the pattern is called a tessellation. A diamond and a hexagon will tessellate, as will any three or four-sided shapes and hexagons. A circle, a star or shapes with curves will not tessellate.

Method for baking biscuits

Pre-heat the oven to 150°C/300°F. Soften the butter and beat in the sugar with a wooden spoon. Sift the flour and mix it into the mixture of butter and sugar, until it becomes a smooth, stiff paste. Dust the board and rolling pin with flour, to ensure the mixture doesn't stick. Roll out the mixture until it is about 3mm thick. Cut out the biscuit shapes. Place them on a greased baking sheet. Cook in the oven for approximately 30 minutes.

Page 20/21

A 2D (flat) shape which can be folded to form a 3D (solid) shape is called a net of the 3D shape. Activities such as opening up boxes and folding nets to make boxes helps children to make the important connections between 2D and 3D shapes. It also helps to reinforce their understanding of the properties of shapes, the perimeter, the shape of the sides etc.

The weighing activity is concerned with comparison. Weighing in the hand is an important starting point. Most young children will use non-standard measures on the weighing scale as units of weight are difficult.

Page 22/23

Sorting everyday objects gives opportunity for counting and discussing. Recognizing the intersection of sets is an important introduction to the recognition of numbers with more than one property e.g., numbers which are 'even' and in the 3 times table. A different symmetry can be created by cutting fruits such as apples across the middle laterally or longitudinally.

Page 24/25

Estimating numbers and amounts when the children cannot see all of them is an important skill. It is helpful to discuss the strategies with the children for making a 'good' guess, e.g. how many sweetcorn seeds can the children see in one row in the illustration? How many rows do they think there will be? So, how many seeds might there be altogether?

Children could use 10 cm and 20 cm strips to help them make the transition from centimetres to metres, when they are using standard measures for length.

Page 26/27

Some children will be familiar with the use of a thermometer to measure body temperature. The concept of negative numbers could also be introduced when discussing the freezing point for water.

The activity for frozen foods reinforces the names of the months. Some children will need to refer back to the calendar on page 24 to check the sequence and names of the months of the year.

A note about computers

If you have access to a simple database with graph facilities, then you can use any of the data collection activities in this book as an opportunity to introduce children to such software. Pie charts can then be used in place of barcharts in certain circumstances. Young children cannot draw pie charts, but they can recognize the relative sizes of the sections.

Index